DEVON
TRANSPORT

This Vulcan ambulance, used by the British Red Cross Society and the St John Ambulance Association during the First World War, was a gift from the Brixham fishermen on 11 March 1916. *(David James)*

BRITAIN IN OLD PHOTOGRAPHS

DEVON TRANSPORT

TED GOSLING

SUTTON PUBLISHING

Sutton Publishing Limited
Phoenix Mill · Thrupp · Stroud
Gloucestershire · GL5 2BU

First published 2006

British Library Cataloguing in Publication Data
A catalogue record for this book is available from the
British Library.

ISBN 0-7509-2949-9

Typeset in 10.5/13.5 Photina.
Typesetting and origination by
Sutton Publishing Limited.
Printed and bound in England by
J.H. Haynes & Co. Ltd, Sparkford.

Title page photograph: The early part of the twentieth century saw a transport revolution that was to change the face of Devon's roads for ever. At that time the motor car was virtually unknown in the county, but by the end of the First World War one of the most revolutionary changes was the coming of the motor bus, which was then known as a charabanc. Here a party is seen at a Dartmoor beauty spot in a fine Lancia coach, *c.* 1925. *(E.S. Gosling collection)*

During the Second World War petrol was strictly rationed and only vehicles on essential work were allowed on the road. Motor fuel ration books with petrol coupons, seen here, were issued to authorise the acquisition of fuel. *(E.S. Gosling collection)*

CONTENTS

Steam roadrollers like this were once a familiar sight in Devon, working on the roads. Today they are sought after by steam enthusiasts like Robin Barnard from the Colyford Motor Museum, seen here giving a polish with an oily rag to a fine Aveling roller. *(Colyford Motor Museum)*

INTRODUCTION

Before the invention of the lorries and cars which now pound their way day and night along our roads, Devon was a county for the horse. From the packhorse trains of the Middle Ages to the lumbering stagecoaches of the early nineteenth century, the horse was supreme and was also the main means of transport for the rider, for private carriages and for horse-drawn carts.

The horse gave employment to a large number of people such as wheelwrights, blacksmiths, saddlers, coachmen, stablemen and grooms. It was a time when most people knew about the horse and were able to discuss the finer points of horsemanship, much as we discuss the cars we drive today. Although the railway brought great changes to Devon life in the nineteenth century, much of the countryman's world still depended on the muscle power of the horse.

The railway was introduced to Devon during the spring of 1844, when the Bristol and Exeter Company completed its line to Exeter. Travelling is more luxurious now than then. The old first-class carriages were tolerable, the second were moderate, and the third were open tubs like cattle wagons, exposed to wind and weather. By 1851 the Devon railway was still confined to the main line from Taunton through Exeter to Plymouth, but over the next fifty years branch lines, controlled more often than not by small independent companies, reached out through the county.

By the turn of the nineteenth century the Great Western Railway and the London and South Western covered Devon, with only a few small lines remaining independent. The last of these was the Teign Valley, which remained in existence until 1923 when the domination of the county by the two great companies was complete.

The coming of the railway contributed much to the development of Devon's seaside towns and, for countless generations of holidaymakers, Exeter became the gateway to their destination. Before reaching Exeter the Southern Railway travelled via Axminster and Honiton, with branch lines pushing down to the seaside resorts of Lyme Regis, Seaton, Sidmouth and Budleigh Salterton through to Exmouth.

Heading down to Plymouth on the old Southern route the train would leave Exeter Central down over the bank and through St David's tunnel into St David's station to follow the western line out to Cowley Bridge Junction. The Southern line would then swing back on the left, passing stations that all railwaymen knew by heart: Newton St Cyres, Crediton, Yeoford, Bow, Meldon Quarry, Bridestowe, Lydford, Brentor, Tavistock North, Bere Alston, Bere Ferrers, Tamerton Foliot Halt, St Budeaux Victoria Road, Devonport Kings Road, Devonport Junction and finally, 58 miles from Exeter, Plymouth North Road.

Two other routes, one to north Devon and the other to north Cornwall, were also operated by the Southern Railway. The train for north Devon would leave Yeoford and take the line at Coleford Junction to travel for just over 42 miles via stations like Copplestone, Morchard Road, Lapford, Eggesford, King's Nympton, Portsmouth Arms, Umberleigh, Chapelton, Barnstaple Junction, Barnstaple Town, Pottington, Wrafton, Braunton, Woolacombe and Mortehoe to arrive at Ilfracombe. The trains for north Cornwall would swing away to the left at Meldon Junction, passing the Meldon viaduct and climbing to over 900ft above sea level (the highest point on the Southern Railway system) for the 60-mile journey to the north Cornwall resort of Padstow; extensions from this line went to Holsworthy and Bude, giving holiday-makers easy access to the north Devon resorts. The main line of the Great Western Railway from Bristol to Penzance went through Tiverton Junction, Exeter St Davids, Newton Abbot and Plymouth, with branch lines to Tiverton and Torbay, the Torbay line reaching as far as Kingswear. Both lines were efficient and safe to use, men were proud to work on them and passengers who travelled on these railways felt a great affection for what must have been a very environmentally friendly system.

The railway network in Devon was to remain virtually intact until the reshaping of the British railways, the Beeching Report of 1963, which advocated closure of most of the branch lines throughout the country. The result was a disaster for Devon.

The first motor cars made their appearance in Devon at the end of the Victorian era and the Motor Car Act of 1903 made the registration of cars compulsory, as was the licensing of drivers. A speed limit of 20mph was also enforced. The increase in

The one long, straight street that runs through Honiton can be seen in this 1930s photograph. The density of traffic had not yet reached the levels which made Honiton traffic jams famous in post-war years. (*Seaton Museum*)

motor traffic was measurable by 1908 and by 1911 there were no fewer than 72,000 registered private cars in use in the UK. By 1939 the car had advanced beyond the wildest dreams of its pioneers and the holidaymakers travelling to Devon by car in those pre-war days would encounter their first traffic jams.

The author, Ted Gosling, who left school in 1943 at the age of fourteen, was born with petrol in his blood, so it was only natural that he would commence his working life serving a five-year apprenticeship as a motor mechanic in a local garage. In those wartime years it was a case of make do and mend to keep vehicles on essential work on the road. Tyres, timing chains and other spares were almost impossible to get. Pool petrol played havoc with exhaust valves and when they burnt out they had to be built up with a welding process called Bright Ray. Ted was fortunate to work in a garage with a good reputation, and although Mr W.L. Oborn, the garage owner, and mechanic Billy Wilkins were hard taskmasters, they taught him all they knew about the motor trade. After the war, at seventeen years of age, he obtained his first driving licence. The driving test had been suspended during the war years and did not return until 1949, so Ted could drive on the road without passing the test. He well remembers the Easter of 1946 when he was just seventeen: Mr Oborn informed him that they were busy that weekend with taxi work, and they wanted him to drive. He was given one driving lesson and let loose on the public. This year he will celebrate sixty years of driving. Things have changed so much from those early days; thanks to the car the silence of the countryside no longer exists, and to ride a horse on the grass verges of Devon roads is now very dangerous. When Ted first started to drive, road rage was unknown and courtesy to other drivers was the order of the day. The number of people killed on Devon roads increases every year. The efficiency of the modern car calls for considerable skill at the wheel, which unfortunately many drivers of all ages lack. As A.C. Hillstead, once a Bentley Boy, observed in *Fifty Years of Motorcars*, 'There is only one person in a thousand today who really knows how to drive.'

Some years before the First World War a Royal Navy torpedo went astray and came up on the beach at Culverhole Point near Rousdon. A Navy team went there to attend to it and G.H. Richards, the Seaton builder, was contracted to convey it to Seaton Hole, where the Navy could get it back aboard the vessel. This picture, with Richards third from the left behind the horse, shows the party about to leave Culverhole Point. The charge for the job, including danger money, was £3. *(E.S. Gosling collection)*

1

When the Horse was Supreme

Before the coming of the motor car no self-respecting doctor with anything of a practice would walk on his rounds. Dr Tonge, the Beer doctor, is seen here with his father, about to set out on his rounds in 1904. The smart turnout was typical for a doctor of his day. (*Seaton Museum*)

When we look at pictures like this we realise that they convey an aura of romance sadly lacking in the cars of today. In the top picture, taken in North Devon before the First World War, we have a governess cart – you could enter these vehicles from behind, making it easier for young children to get aboard. In the bottom picture is a smart two-wheel gig, which at the time of this picture, *c.* 1920, was about the equivalent of the present-day Mini. *(Seaton Museum)*

Before the end of the Edwardian period Devon was still the kingdom of the horse. In the top picture a party makes a stop at the Three Horseshoes, near Sidmouth. *c.* 1909.

In the picture on the left, taken in about 1910, Harry Clapp is pictured driving a party to the Colcombe Castle Hotel in Colyton. *(E.S. Gosling collection)*

Awliscombe, c. 1885. This fine photograph shows what the roads were like in East Devon before motor traffic. Today the road through the village has become a busy feeder-route to the M5 motorway, but in the late Victorian period it was just a muddy, untarred road. The star of this picture is undoubtedly the fine timber wagon parked at the side of the road. (E.S. Gosling collection)

Opposite, top: Fore Street, Sidmouth, c. 1901. The omnibus office of J. Lake and Son can be seen to the right of this photograph. The Lakes owned a livery establishment and the people standing outside their booking office could have been waiting for the horse-drawn station bus. Up to this date most coaches, including the famous 'Defiance' and 'Telegraph', left here for their destinations. (Seaton Museum)

Opposite, bottom: Before the age of the car, most people travelled to Devon by rail. Unless your destination was close to a station it would have been necessary to cover some distance on the road. There were then two possibilities: you walked, or you used the town bus, which was drawn by horse. Thomas Clapp of Seaton is pictured here, standing in front of his Seaton Town Bus, which would have met all local trains. (E.S. Gosling collection)

By the end of the nineteenth century the design and appearance of horse-drawn vehicles reached heights of excellence which are demonstrated in this photograph of a horse-drawn bus arriving at its Devon destination, *c. 1899. (D. Harman-Young)*

Before the advent of the tractor Devon farmers used horse power to work on the land. Grass for hay is ready for mowing in June and this Devon farmer is turning the grass on his horse-drawn rake, to expose the maximum area to air and sunlight. *(E.S. Gosling collection)*

The horse-drawn milk float was very much a part of everyday life before the Second World War. I always thought they looked like a latter-day version of Boadicea's war chariot – built very low to the ground, with two large wheels. Ornate sign boards at the front and sides advertise the name of the dairyman. The highly polished churns were placed in the cart, and customers had milk served into their jugs by a dipper. In the top picture we have Mr Thomas from Seaton, ready to leave for his milk round, *c.* 1920. In the bottom picture milkman Jack Loud can be seen busy on his morning round, *c.* 1913. *(E.S. Gosling collection)*

Royal Glen Hotel, Sidmouth, 1887. This splendid four-in-hand with a coachload of passengers must have formed some part of Queen Victoria's Golden Jubilee celebrations. The Royal Glen was built in 1809 and it was here, just before Christmas 1819, that the Duke and Duchess of Kent stayed with their seven-month-old daughter, the future Queen. While here the young princess had a narrow escape when a boy shooting sparrows in the road outside broke a window with a bullet, which just grazed the baby princess's sleeve. *(E.S. Gosling collection)*

Clapps Transport, Seaton, *c.* 1912. The pair of horses and wagonette driven by Harry Clapp is leaving Manor Road for the Lamberts Castle races. These races attracted thousands of spectators, and Clapp was the last driver with horses to attend after motor coaches replaced the old way of travel. *(E.S. Gosling collection)*

Although popular as children's pets and for work at the seaside, donkeys have never been used extensively in Devon for farm work. They were, however, used by the Branscombe cliff farmers, who grew early potatoes. The two seen here with panniers on their backs were on their way to the cliffs to load up, *c.* 1926. (*Seaton Museum*)

Before the twentieth century in Devon the horse reigned supreme, and travelling on horseback was the norm. However, by the early 1920s it became obvious that the day of the horse, except for a limited number kept for pleasure, had passed. Here in the 1950s, on Sidmouth sea front, we have horses kept for just that use, with visitors enjoying a ride on a fine summer day. (*E.S.Gosling collection*)

Clovelly is one of Devon's showpieces, and that it remains well preserved and unspoilt is thanks to the Lords of the Manor, the Hamlyns. Cars are not allowed, and so steep and narrow is the High Street that the locals name the road Up-along or Down-along. Before the 1950s donkeys were used to carry visitors down to the harbour. They can be seen in this 1938 photograph carrying tourists Up-along. (*Seaton Museum*)

Devon man Walt Peach proudly stands in front of his draught horse, *c.* 1930. The noble horse still gave employment to a tremendous number of people in the county, and Peach must have devoted hours to polishing, cleaning and furbishing this animal and its harness to obtain such a smart turnout. (*E.S. Gosling collection*)

We all know the song about Widecombe Fair that tells how Tom Cobley and a group of friends borrowed a mare and came across the moor to Widecombe. Are these young ladies re-enacting that event? East Devon, 1930. *(E.S. Gosling collection)*

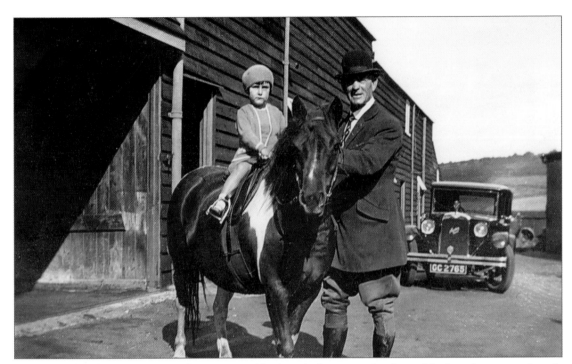

Her first riding lesson, *c.* 1930. The young girl looks a little uncertain about this, but she was quite safe in the capable hands of Harry Clapp, well-known East Devon horseman. *(E.S. Gosling collection)*

For your final ride, what better way to depart than in a splendid horse-drawn hearse. James Leyman, the builder responsible for the Highwell Road development in Seaton, died in 1925, and in this photograph you can see his funeral cortège leaving the road he built. *(E.S. Gosling collection)*

2

Devon Railways

Brixham station, *c*. 1960. Class 1400 engines were used on the
branch line, which closed for passenger service on 13 May 1963, under
the Beeching Report. *(David James)*

A fine picture of the railway engine *Prince*, which was used on the Brixham branch line, *c.* 1880. *(David James)*

The Brixham branch train waits in the bay platform at Churston, *c.* 1950. The Links Hotel is in the background. The Torbay line extended to the Kingswear terminus in 1864, and the little Brixham branch from Churston opened in 1868. *(David James)*

The south line between Exeter and Newton Abbot was opened on 31 December 1846, and passengers between there and Torquay were conveyed by coach. Within two years the line to Torre was open for traffic, and the opening ceremony in December 1848 was observed as a holiday. As usual, the poor were feasted, the inhabitants dined together and marched in procession to the railway station, flags waved and a good time was had by all. The romance of steam disappeared in the 1950s, and here you can see the first diesel on the Torbay Express in 1959. *(E.S. Gosling collection)*

Sidmouth Junction station, looking west towards Exeter. Note the level crossing gates in the distance. This was the junction for Sidmouth branch and also the Exmouth branch, which went via Tipton St John and Budleigh Salterton. Sidmouth Junction was 159 miles and 22 chains from Waterloo. (*Seaton Museum*)

Exeter Central station, *c.* 1962. Rebuilt Merchant Navy Class no. 35013 *Blue Funnel* can be seen in charge of the 12.30 p.m. Up 'Atlantic Coast Express'. (*M. Clement*)

A chapter of events caused this derailment at the Down siding at Seaton Junction during November 1929. A steam breakdown crane from Exmouth Junction shed is seen here lifting N Class 2–6–0 mixed traffic engine no. 1829, which went over the bank during shunting duties. Apparently the engine went up the dead-end siding instead of out on to the main line, and was unable to stop. The shunter gave the signalman the wrong bell, the signalman pulled the wrong points and the engine crew didn't check the ground signal before moving the engine. *(E.S. Gosling collection)*

The London & South Western Railway reached Exeter in 1860, with a new station under Northernhay, in Queen Street. The years that followed became a period of competition between the London & South Western and the Great Western Railway, who had their station in St David's. With both lines passing through the city the advantages to Exeter were many, and for generations of holidaymakers Exeter became the gateway to Devon. Queen Street station was rebuilt in 1933 and renamed Exeter Central, seen here in 1958. *(M. Clement collection)*

Exmouth Junction shed. Approximately 140 locomotives were allocated to Exmouth Junction shed, with over 400 men employed to their needs. The shed, three-quarters of a mile from Exeter Central, was a busy place during the peak summer months when the two disposal roads and the cooling plant would be full up. The shed was finally closed on 6 March 1967. In this picture, from about 1951, an unrebuilt Merchant Navy on shed, displaying the 'Devon Belle' headboard, keeps company with West Country Class no. 34021 *Dartmoor*. *(M. Clement collection)*

Opposite, top: The Down 'Atlantic Coast Express' to Plymouth runs into Okehampton station hauled by West Country class no. 34030 *Watersmeet*, October 1949. The 'Atlantic Coast Express' ran daily from 1927 in both directions under the Southern Railway until the end of the summer service in 1964 when the Western Region took over control of the line west of Salisbury. During the height of the summer season the 'Atlantic Coast Express' ran in three portions – the Plymouth, the North Devon and the North Cornwall – and was full of holidaymakers. *(M. Clement collection)*

Opposite, bottom: Exeter Central platform 4, 18 July 1958. Drummond 0–4–4 M7 tank no. 30044 waits to depart for the Exmouth branch line. Exmouth is 10½ miles by rail from Exeter and the journey included stops at Topsham, Woodbury and Lympstone. Then 4 miles out of Exeter the train would draw up at Topsham and would travel along the river bank enabling passengers to admire the scenery. At the turn of the century there were about twenty trains daily each way between Exeter and Exmouth, including a special express which left Exmouth in the morning and returned from Exeter in the evening. *(M. Clement collection)*

Having worked the 'Atlantic Coast Express' down from Waterloo, unrebuilt Merchant Navy class no. 35024 *East Asiatic Company*, with two engines behind, stands on the disposal road at Exmouth Junction shed. During the locomotive's visit to Exmouth Junction shed the fire would have been cleaned and made up, and the smoke box and ash pan cleaned. It would then be recoaled and watered to be turned on the table ready for a run back to Waterloo. The two white discs on the front indicate Exeter Central and Exmouth Junction. *(M. Clement)*

Photographer Derek Cross managed to capture something of the private working world of the railways with this fine period picture taken in July 1958. A stone train with ballast from Meldon Quarry is climbing up the last bit of the ¼ mile curving 1 in 37 bank from Exeter St Davids to Exeter Central. The train, hauled by an N class, has topped the summit with two E1/R 0–6–0 tank engines as bankers bringing up the rear. The limestone and granite quarries at Meldon were 2½ miles south-west of Okehampton. Meldon Viaduct is a notable piece of railway engineering carrying the railway over a deep ravine of 160ft. *(M. Clement)*

Opposite, bottom: Axminster station, 1961. The station lay to the south-west of the town centre, on the old L&SWR route from Waterloo to Exeter. The station platforms were connected by a covered footbridge. Note the Lyme Regis branch train in the bay platform, waiting for passengers. *(E.S. Gosling collection)*

The Cannington Viaduct, pictured here under construction in 1902, was the most famous part of the Axminster–Lyme Regis branch line. With a maximum height of 93ft above the valley floor, the viaduct was a major engineering feat. Construction was assisted by an aerial cableway that stretched across the valley, and can be plainly seen in this picture. Built of concrete, the viaduct was 203yd long and supported on ten elliptical arches. Owing to shifting quicksands, the third arch from the Axminster end had to be strengthened by the addition of a jack arch soon after it opened. In the early days of the line speed over the Cannington Viaduct was restricted to 15mph, but this was later increased to 25mph. *(E.S. Gosling collection)*

For ninety-eight years thousands of passengers used the branch line at Seaton. Excited holidaymakers arrived and left, people travelled to and from work, businessmen left for appointments and men from Seaton and Colyford went off to war. Year after year the pageant swept in some fresh form along the metalled track, until that sad day when a great silence fell upon the line. Here we see Seaton station, pictured a few years after the 1966 closure. (*E.S. Gosling collection*)

Passengers at Budleigh Salterton waiting for a train to arrive, 1925. Like most seaside towns, Budleigh Salterton owes much of its development to the railway. The building of the railway line to Budleigh Salterton from a junction at Tipton St John was commemorated with a ceremony of cutting the first sod. The line opened on 15 May 1897, and this branch line from Exmouth that ran to Sidmouth Junction lasted for sixty-four years. (*Seaton Museum*)

With an absorbing passion for using their cameras on anything and everything, pre-war photographers have left behind a rich legacy of pictures. Engine no. 1439 is seen here at Brixham station in the old GWR days. The fireman is leaning out of the cab, and the engine driver, standing outside, is holding an oil can. The other two men are station staff. *(David James)*

Opposite, top: Axminster station opened on 19 July 1860. In this picture we have a West Country Class no. 34032 *Camelford* passing through the station a hundred years later in August 1960. *(E.S. Gosling collection)*

Opposite, bottom: Seaton station, *c.* 1910. Note the gas lamp standard. *(E.S. Gosling collection)*

The opening, in March 1868, of the branch line of the L&SWR from Colyton Junction (as it was first called) marked a big step forward for the East Devon area. Colyton Junction soon became Seaton Junction, and remained open for nearly 100 years, closing on 5 March 1966. The top picture is a detailed view of Seaton Junction, taken in 1961. In the lower picture, looking west towards Honiton Bank, *c.* 1956, you can see a S15 Class on an Up stopping train. *(E.S. Gosling collection)*

The locomotive *Seaton*, pictured here in about 1950, was a Light Pacific of the West Country class, no. 21C120. *(E.S. Gosling collection)*

Seaton station, *c.* 1957. The opening in March 1868 of the Seaton branch line of the L&SWR marked a big step forward in the history of the town. The journey from Seaton Junction down the 4 miles to Seaton passed Colyton and Colyford, following the valley of the Axe to stop short of the sea. The station seen here was rebuilt after the branch closure in 1966. The taxis seen waiting at the station belonged to Clapps Transport. *(E.S. Gosling collection)*

In store at Exmouth Junction shed, standing in one of the little-used roads behind the coal hopper, are Drummond 0–6–0 goods engines of the 700 class, nos. 30689–30697, fitted with snow ploughs, 17 July 1962. In a few months' time, following the blizzard of 27 December 1962, these engines would be in frequent use. There were no further snowfalls to rival the one of 27 December, but Arctic conditions remained throughout January and February 1963, making this the most severe winter since 1740. It was during this winter, when the snow remained for over sixty days, that these engines were used over the Plymouth line on Dartmoor. The enginemen who worked them gave them the name of 'Black Motors'. (*M. Clement*)

Opposite: The eastern approaches to Exeter Central station were spacious and level with the typical modern Southern layout. During July 1958 West Country class 4–6–2 no. 34035 *Shaftesbury* passes Exeter Central 'A' box with an Exeter to Salisbury local, while Battle of Britain class no. 34056 *Croydon* runs into the south side of the station with a Down express. With Exeter Central as its focal point the old London & South Western dominated Devon and a great rivalry existed between it and the Great Western Railway. All this was to change after the nationalisation of railways in 1948, and by the time of this picture a decade later British Railways had come into being. The passing of the two railway companies at midnight on 31 December 1947 was a sad day for many of the older railwaymen who took great pride in the individuality of their companies. Worse was to follow with the BR modernisation plan of 1955 and the Beeching Report of 1963, which resulted in the reduction of route mileage from nearly 20,000 to 12,500 miles. (*M. Clement*)

The Southern Railway vigorously promoted Devon as a holiday destination, and provided trains such as the 'Devon Belle', seen here on 8 July 1949. The 'Devon Belle' was introduced in June 1947 to run between Waterloo, Plymouth and Ilfracombe. During the early years the 'Belle' was often loaded to fourteen coaches, totalling some 550 tons. The train, which ceased running in September 1954, was made up entirely of Pullman cars. In this picture, the Down 'Devon Belle' passes by the coal hopper at Exmouth Junction shed, with unrebuilt Merchant Navy Pacific no. 35007 *Aberdeen Commonwealth* in charge. *(M. Clement)*

3

Journeys by Tram

April 1882 saw a stretch of horse-drawn tramway operating between St Sidwells and Heavitree in Exeter, with the line from St David's station to the Blackboy turnpike opening the following year. The venture was not a great success, and by the beginning of the twentieth century it was decided that an overhead system of electric traction should be adopted. This is one of the horse-drawn trams, *c.* 1898.
(R. Richards)

The first horse-drawn tram in Plymouth ran on 17 March 1872, ten years before Exeter had one, and these were replaced by an electric tramway system on 22 September 1899. The last tram in Plymouth ran on Saturday 29 September 1945, from Old Town Street to Peverell, amid tremendous crowds. In the top picture we have a Plymouth Corporation tram and in the lower photograph a Corporation bus stands next to a tram car. *(R. Richards)*

Trams were the ideal medium for advertising and, in an intensely competitive market, placing your brand on the side of a moving vehicle proved rewarding. The Plymouth tram pictured here in about 1914 carries a conspicuous sign advertising Hardings Furnishing Arcades in Union Street. (R. Richards)

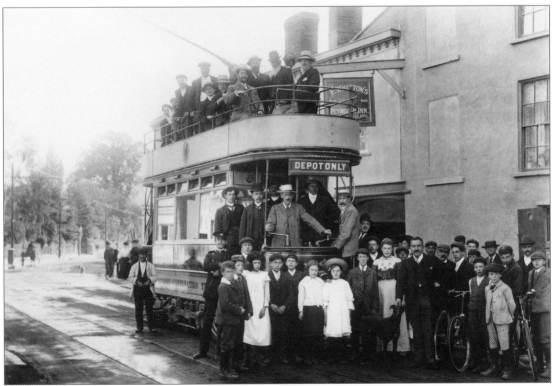

A fine picture of Exeter tram car no. 4, which was built in 1905. The photograph was taken outside the Plymouth Arms in Alphington, c. 1906. (R. Richards)

Before 1931 there were three tram routes in Exeter: Alphington Road via Exe Bridge and the High Street to Pinhoe Road; Cowick Street via Exe Bridge, High Street and Paris Street to Church Terrace, Heavitree; and Queen Street at the junction with High Street, via the Clock Tower down to St David's station. In the top picture we have an attractive view of an Edwardian Exeter Corporation tram, and in the lower picture a tram can be seen passing the Guildhall in the High Street, *c*. 1908. *(R. Richards)*

The first electric tram in Devon had run in Plymouth in 1899. Exeter followed in 1905 and the only other Devon town to have a tramway system was Torquay. They were never generally loved, the rails became a menace to the cyclist and they could only operate in towns and cities. In the end it was the superior manoeuvrability of the motor bus that finally overcame them, but today many people regard tram cars as a romantic form of travel. This photograph shows one of Exeter's first electric trams, in the High Street bound for Heavitree. There is no date on the photograph, but the clothing of the pedestrians seems to place it in the Edwardian period. *(R. Richards)*

The new electric tramway system in Exeter was inaugurated in April 1905, and at first proved successful, with over three million passengers carried in the first year of operation. By 1931 the trams were replaced by trolley buses, which did not prove popular in the city, and they were eventually replaced by motor buses. Exeter tram cars nos 9 and 4 can be seen in this photograph, *c.* 1910. *(R. Richards)*

SEATON TRAMWAY

The unique Seaton Tramway draws tens of thousands of visitors every year, making it one of Devon's most popular attractions. It's all a far cry from what began as one man's hobby over fifty years ago. That hobby turned into a dream and the dream has endured into a new century.

The origins can be traced back to Claude Lane's Lancaster Electrical Company in Barnet, north London, which built battery electric vehicles such as milk floats in the 1940s. But Lane's real passion was trams, and the factory helped him realise his ambition of constructing a 15in-gauge tram based on ex-Darwen Car 23, running on the Llandudno and Colwyn Bay system.

Claude began running his creation at fêtes and similar local events and he was soon taken aback by its popularity. It led to a one-off summer season at St Leonards in Sussex in 1951 and five years at Rhyl from 1952. These successes persuaded Claude to negotiate a lease on a permanent site at Eastbourne in 1953.

The project flourished and several more trams were added to the fleet. But by the 1960s the growth of Eastbourne's traffic system began to threaten the tramway's position. So Claude Lane looked elsewhere for a longer-term, more secure home for his pride and joy.

Along the south coast British Rail was about to close the Seaton to Seaton Junction branch line as part of the Beeching plan. It was finally shut down in 1966. Claude Lane opened negotiations with BR and a public inquiry into his plans was held. Some participants claimed the tramway would create unacceptable noise and spoil the natural beauty of the Axe Valley, but the local council believed it would become an asset.

Permission was finally granted for the tramway in 1969. The job of dismantling the system in Eastbourne and taking it to Seaton for the 1970 season fell almost wholly to Claude Lane and his assistant Allan Gardner. They made some thirty-six return lorry journeys virtually round the clock and built the Riverside Depot. The track laying began immediately.

Car 8 became the first tram to run in passenger service on 28 August 1970. With no overhead cables at that time, power was taken from a battery wagon towed by the tram. That winter, activity centred on the regauging of the tram bogies to 2ft 9in gauge, and the erecting of poles to carry overhead wire.

Before the eagerly anticipated 1971 season could open Claude Lane suffered a heart attack, dying in April of that year. Allan Gardner took over as managing director with the backing of the Lane family, and a nucleus of volunteers who knew of the company's plight offered their enthusiastic help. Everyone was determined to see the project through as its founder would have wanted.

Months and years of hard work followed. Passing loops were installed; the first tram powered by the overhead cable ran in 1973; the line was extended to the terminus in the town centre's Harbour Road car park in 1975; and the final extension to Colyton was completed by 1980. The fleet grew and grew.

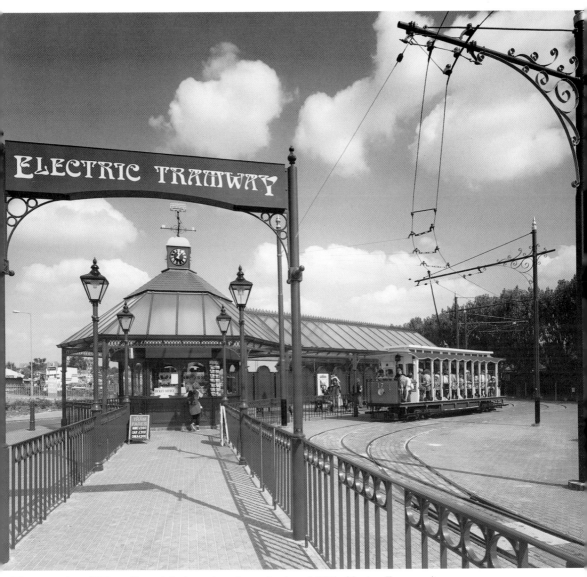

The sensational Edwardian-style tram terminus, Seaton, 1995. *(Seaton Tramway)*

The company's 25th Anniversary at Seaton was marked by the construction of a new Edwardian-style terminus, now a prominent landmark in the town. The following year Colyton station underwent a facelift and the Riverside Depot was extended shortly afterwards.

Today Seaton Tramway is expanding and more than 90,000 visitors a year are discovering its magic. Claude Lane's dream is thriving. He would have been proud.

Running parallel with the Seaton Marshes, trams pass on the Axmouth loop, *c.* 1985. (*Seaton Tramway*)

Car 12 after the 1999 rebuild, seen at the Seaton Terminus. (*Seaton Tramway*)

Car 8, *c*. 1973. Note that although the overhead poles were in situ the cables were not yet connected, and the power for no. 8 came from a battery wagon towed by the tram. (*Seaton Museum*)

No. 12, pictured here going into the Axmouth loop, was built in 1966 at Eastbourne. Originally an enclosed single-decker as seen here, it was rebuilt as an open-topper in 1980. It was again rebuilt in 1999, the more enclosed design resembling the London Feltham trams of the 1930s. (*Seaton Museum*)

South of Bobsworth Bridge, no. 7 returns to the Seaton Terminus, *c.* 1978. Car 7 was built in 1958 at Barnet, based on the ex-Bournemouth open-toppers of the Llandudno and Colwyn Bay system. (*Seaton Museum*)

Nos 8, 2 and 12 are seen here in 1972. Car 8 was built in 1968 at Eastbourne. It was the first car to be built for the Seaton gauge of 2ft 9in. Tram 2 was also built at Eastbourne and was based on the London Metropolitan Tramways type A design. (*Seaton Museum*)

Allan Gardner in charge of car 17, with staff members aboard. No. 17 was built in 1988 at Seaton, based on the Manx Electric Railway 'toast rack' cars. Removable seats allowed wheelchairs to be carried. (*Seaton Tramway*)

At the time of this picture the tramway ended at the Colyford crossing, seen here in 1975. (*Seaton Tramway*)

4

Journeys by Coach

It was during the Edwardian period that William Albert Dagworthy (1873–1951), realising the importance of the automobile, changed from repairing horse-drawn vehicles to servicing cars and opened the first garage in Sidmouth. Dagworthy is pictured here some time before the First World War, with one of his fine charabancs.
(Seaton Museum)

The highlight of a day out in a charabanc was the stop for the midday meal, and pubs in accessible places popular with day trippers quickly expanded the range of their menus. The people seen here on Dartmoor in 1931 belonged to a coach party that had stopped for lunch at the Warren House Inn. (*E.S. Gosling collection*)

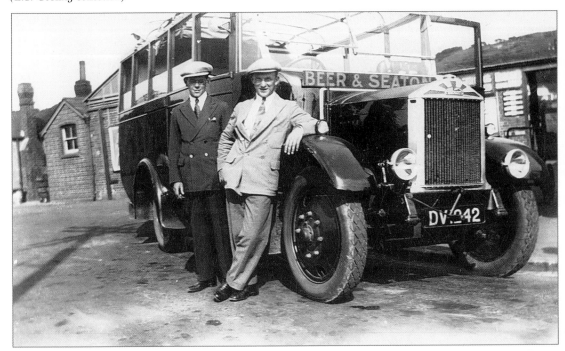

A fine Albion Motor Bus used in the East Devon area, *c.* 1929. By the time of this picture motor buses like this were beginning to figure on the Devon transport scene. (*Seaton Museum*)

The charabanc became popular in the 1920s. At first they were open to the elements and short on comfort, but by the 1930s they were to acquire protection against the weather and graduated into motor coaches. In the top picture we have a charabanc, *c.* 1924, which had made a stop outside a pub in a Devon seaside resort – no doubt the party of men on board were looking forward to a drink. The bottom picture was taken in 1932. By this date vehicles like Clapps Parlour Coaches had become more sophisticated. *(E.S. Gosling collection)*

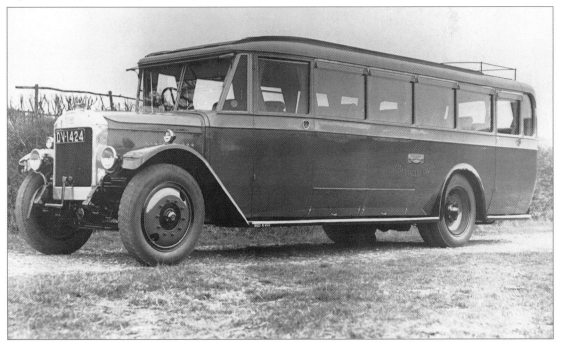

Seaton Gospel Hall members on a day trip to the Cheddar Caves, *c.* 1927. The pleasure of a day out in a charabanc is reflected in their faces. Few people had cars in those days, and destinations like the Cheddar Caves were inaccessible to most people. *(E.S. Gosling collection)*

The distance from Totnes to Dartmouth by river is about 8 miles, and visitors flock to Dartmouth or Totnes for the excursion on the Dart. The men seen in this charabanc in about 1925 were leaving Exeter to join a paddle steamer for the River Dart trip and to enjoy some of the finest scenery in Devon. *(E.S. Gosling collection)*

Although Royal Blue Coaches, with their distinctive style, were the main operators, with services from London's Victoria coach station to all Devon resorts, Arthur Good also ran a service in the 1920s from London via Staines, Salisbury, Dorchester and Lyme Regis to Seaton and Beer, with his Silver Cars. Good's Silver Cars operated from Station Road, Seaton, and the Leland Cub coach seen here at Cheddar during June 1933 was used on this service. *(J. Hooper)*

In Devon, buses were an important means of transport during the war, with conductresses helping to keep the transport moving. *(J. Hooper)*

Members of the Women's Meeting, Seaton Gospel Hall, had a narrow escape when, on a coach outing, the vehicle left the road and slid into a ditch. Apart from the shock, no-one was hurt, and here we see some of the party discussing the event, *c.* 1965. *(E.S. Gosling collection)*

This splendid Guy coach belonged to Brixham coach operators Burton's. It was caught on camera on 7 August 1952, en route to Berry Head. *(David James)*

The Victorians may have been the first to declare 'We do like to be beside the seaside', but for many holidaymakers the arrival of the charabanc early in the last century brought a new type of holiday – the classic tour, criss-crossing the country and linking resorts. At the vanguard of these new tour operations in Devon was Greenslades, named after its founder and launched before the First World War. Here we have a fine AEC coach from Greenslade Tours in Bank Lane, Brixham, with Brixham bus station in the background. *(David James)*

This Grey Car motor coach operated a service from Paignton and Churston to Brixham during the 1920s. The passengers are wearing a variety of hats. I wonder – did they all stay on when the driver got his charabanc up to 20mph, or was it a case of numerous stops to retrieve lost headgear? *(David James)*

During the heyday of Greenslade Tours of Exeter the firm arranged a full programme of continental tours. These tourists from the West Country, making a stop to explore in Holland, had just left the fine AEC Continental coach seen on the left of the photograph. *(E.S. Gosling collection)*

A Bedford service bus belonging to Burton's of Brixham is seen outside the local bus station, loading passengers for the holiday camps and the Castor Estate, *c.* 1960. *(David James)*

This coach, which belonged to Burton's, was used on the Kingswear to Paignton route during the 1960s. *(David James)*

This Ford Bellhouse Hartwell coach was used by Down's Motors of Ottery St Mary in the late 1950s; this photograph dates from 1960. At a later date this coach was fully restored and featured in the TV series *Heartbeat*. *(Down's Motors)*

Down's Motors of Ottery St Mary operate a coach service trading under the name of Otter Coaches. The coach pictured here with two children standing in front, in about 1970, was a Guy coach with a Mulliner body; only two of this type were made. *(Down's Motors)*

The Guy coach with the Mulliner body, belonging to Down's Motors, *c.* 1970. *(Down's Motors)*

A fine Western National Bristol double-decker bus at a Devon Bus Rally, 8 June 1996. *(Seaton Tramway)*

Winner of a Green Tourist award in 2003/05, Round Robin River Link provides bus departures daily to and from Paignton and Totnes Steamer Quay, for the River Link cruises to Dartmouth. The river cruise on the Dart attracts thousands of visitors every year, and, in the top picture, passengers from a river cruise board a bus at Totnes Steamer Quay. In the bottom picture, also taken at the Steamer Quay, stands a fine Bristol VRT Series 3 bus, used on the River Link service. (*River Link*)

For generations of visitors to Devon, Royal Blue coaches were as much a part of life in the county as the Great Western Railway. Founded in 1880 in Bournemouth by Thomas Elliot, the company originally operated horse-drawn transport. Following the First World War rapid expansion took place, and the gleaming dark blue and cream livery of the motor coaches became synonymous with long-distance travel. By the 1930s Royal Blue were running journeys from London to Exeter, Minehead, Weymouth and other towns in the West Country. After the Second World War the company had to cope with large numbers of passengers, especially on Saturdays during the summer season, and employed local coach companies such as Greenslade Tours to help out. Ted Gosling, who worked as a driver for Greenslades in about 1959, well remembers following the Royal Blue driver with his relief coach on the Exmouth to Victoria Coach Station, London, service. Royal Blue drivers were then kings of the road and young Ted had his work cut out trying to keep up with them. By 1990 the writing was on the wall, and the famous Royal Blue name was dropped. Royal Blue vehicles can still be seen in nostalgic rallies of restored coaches and this Royal Blue was present at a bus rally in Bristol, 23 August 1993. *(R. Richards)*

Fred Diment's Garage, Station Road, Seaton, *c.* 1908. Diment opened the first garage in Seaton in 1905.
The premises were in Station Road (now Harbour Road), and he was the agent for Sunbeam and
Star cars. The business was bought in 1909 by Ben Trevett, who lived with his family in the adjoining
house. His son George took over the garage in 1936, and ran the business until his retirement in
1978. George Trevett, who died in 1985, was involved in many of the sporting activities of the town.
(E.S. Gosling collection)

5

The Mechanical Horse

A scene in Fore Street, Hartland, *c.* 1930. Motor traffic today has brought many disadvantages to town and country life, and this typical street scene of the time reminds us how quiet the roads were then. *(E.S. Gosling collection)*

This 1926 Bullnose Morris appears to have taken part in a carnival procession. The picture was taken in 1930 at an unknown venue in North Devon, and the occupants of the car appear to be enjoying themselves. *(E.S. Gosling collection)*

Somewhere on Dartmoor, a proud owner stands beside the Sunbeam saloon car, a thoroughbred if ever there was one, at a time before the company was taken over by Rootes. *(J. Hooper)*

Townsend Garage, Beer

Cars for Hire

W. L. OBORN, Proprietor

Michelin Stockists

The Leading Garage for Repairs in Beer

MOTOR REPAIRS
PETROL & OILS
WIRELESS

Electrical Fittings and Lamps
Supplied

Mr W.L. Oborn founded the Townsend Garage in Beer in 1922, and was still very much involved in the business when he died in the 1970s, aged eighty-two. With his two sons, Stanley and Gerald, he gave a first-class service to all motorists, and the name Oborn became a by-word for integrity. The advertisements shown here date back to the 1920s. *(Norman Lambert)*

With Compliments from

W. L. Oborn & Sons

TOWNSEND GARAGE

SPARES

MOTOR
ENGINEERS

BEER · · S. DEVON
(Above the Schools)

ACCESSORIES

TYRES

TAXIS

BATTERIES

CAR SALES

INSURANCE

Personal Attention 1905 *Tel. No. Seaton 59*

By the 1920s the number of small and cheap cars in Devon, very largely used for pleasure, meant an increased demand for petrol and oil, with roadside garages meeting calls for spare parts and repairs. The garage seen in the top picture, in Mill Street, Ottery St Mary, in about 1925, was then named East Devon Motors, and at that time petrol was still supplied to the motorist in two-gallon cans. In the bottom picture is the same garage in 1960 – the name had changed to Down's Motors, and petrol pumps with swing arms over the pavement can be seen. *(Down's Motors)*

To Devon in style. This fine Vauxhall Prince Henry model of 1911 was an Edwardian car of the highest class, and the first real British sports car. *(Colyford Motor Museum)*

A rare car in Devon, this fine Hupmobile tourer was caught on camera in Plymouth, *c.* 1927. Most people under sixty in this country today have never heard of a Hupmobile. The company, founded by Robert and Louis Hupp in Detroit, produced fine cars in the medium-price range, and were in production from 1908 to 1941. (*Colyford Motor Museum*)

Opposite, top: The unmetalled roads of Devon, with loose stones and dust, were hazards for pioneering Edwardian motorists. Judging by the appearance of this fine car, it had not yet encountered any such road surface. (*Colyford Motor Museum*)

Opposite, bottom: Motor cars first made their appearance in East Devon in about 1901, and it is believed that the very first belonged to garage owner Fred Diment. That car is pictured here on Seaton Regatta Day, *c.* 1906. Apparently there was widespread excitement when Fred really gave the car the works and reached speeds of 20mph! (*E.S. Gosling collection*)

Colyford Filling Station was built in 1928, and became a symbol of what a tidy site could look like. It was described in an early planning publication as 'an ideal design for the county of Devon'. The Davey family ran the filling station until 1975 when Mr and Mrs Davey retired and sold the site. Robin Barnard purchased the filling station in 1982 from the owner who had failed to give the community the service which Mr and Mrs Davey offered. The filling station was closed in recent years, but the petrol pumps were restored as a part of the Motoring Memories museum. In the picture on the left a fine MG awaits the friendly attended service, *c.* 1990. In the bottom picture a van advertises the museum.
(Colyford Motor Museum)

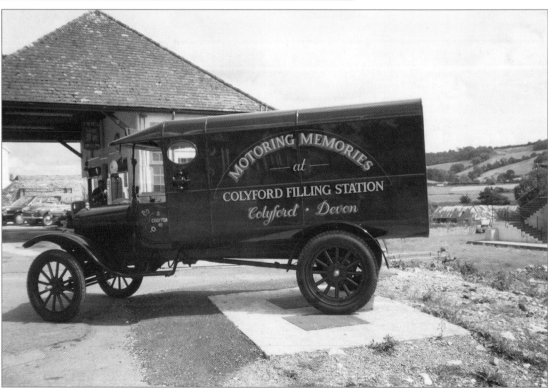

In 1922 Herbert Austin unveiled to the press a car just 8ft 9in long and 3ft 10in wide, with a 696cc engine, with the quote 'a decent car for the man who at present can only afford a motor cycle and sidecar'. The Baby Austin went on sale in 1923 and the public bought it and loved it. The engine was soon uprated to 747cc and the car became known as the Chummy. In the top picture Beer garage owner W.L. Oborn is sitting in a 1920 Chummy. In the bottom picture, again taken in Beer, is the distinctive Austin Seven, *c.* 1938. *(G. Oborn)*

Today the possession of a fine Sunbeam car is the hallmark of a true vintage car enthusiast. Here, however, we return to 1927, when W.L. Oborn, the East Devon garage owner, was on tour in Europe and stopped to take this photograph of the Sunbeam Tourer he was driving. *(G. Oborn)*

Fresh air motoring *c.* 1906. A family from Devon were snapped by the camera while touring Scotland in this aristocratic Lanchester. *(G. Oborn)*

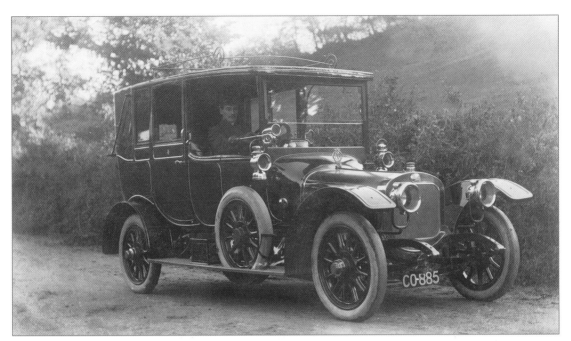

This fine Sunbeam landaulet, seen near Barnstaple in North Devon, is a thoroughbred if ever there was one. Sunbeam cars had a first-rate reputation and the company had one of the most famous names in motoring history. *(G. Oborn)*

Blackler's General Stores, Middle Street, Brixham, *c.* 1925. The car parked in the street outside the Stores is a Model T Ford. With tongue-in-cheek humour it was said that the Model T could be bought in ten shades of black, or that 'a piece of tin with a length of cord – join them together and you get a Ford'. *(David James)*

The Standard Vanguard was introduced in 1947. Its 2.1-litre engine was also used in the Triumph, the Morgan Plus Four and the Ferguson tractor of its time. With several body restyles, the Vanguard went on until 1961. The Vanguard seen here, with owner Wilf Winnett from Colyton, was tackling the heavy snowdrifts near Bovey House, Beer, during the severe winter of 1963. (*Seaton Museum*)

Ted Gosling is seen here in a 1954 TF MG., *c.* 1960. This car, belonging to Ted, only had the Nuffield engine of 1250cc, and the top speed, with difficulty, was about 80mph – the optional 1466cc unit gave the car a little more power. The TF was the last of the traditional, much loved series, and was very attractive, with sporty looks. (*E.S. Gosling collection*)

The Humber car company built cars in Coventry, and the pre-war Super Snipe was equipped with four individual seats plus two tip-up seats at the back. Ted Gosling is seen here in 1959 with a Humber Snipe which he purchased for £20. Note the Singer next to the Humber – he had purchased this car for £4. *(E.S. Gosling collection)*

Two cars which were once a part of Ted Gosling's stable: on the left a fully restored Bullnose Morris, 1925, and to the right an open tourer Humber, pre-1930. *(E.S. Gosling collection)*

Trevetts Garage, Harbour Road, Seaton, *c. 1937*. Trevetts traded successfully for over sixty years. During that time it gave employment to over one hundred people in the town. The staff members here are, left to right, Ralph Anning (Ralph came from Colyford and died of fever in Africa during the Second World War), Stanley Parker (Axmouth), Alec Parr (Colyford), Horace Clark (foreman, Seaton), Dick Iles (Colyton), Bert Williams (Seaton). *(E.S. Gosling collection)*

Central Garage, Seaton, *c. 1929*. Central Garage stood on the site of the present post office sorting office. Standing next to the car in the garage is a well-known Seatonian, Mr Bob Hoskins, who died in about 1980. *(E.S. Gosling collection)*

A Mini struggles through the snow at Broadclyst after a snowfall in January 1963. A boxy little car of unitary construction, the Mini was new in almost every way. It was the creation of Alec Issigonis, and the suspension was developed by Alex Moulton. The Mini epitomised the 'swinging sixties', the era of hippies and a revolution in dress. When Paddy Hopkirk and Henry Liddon drove a Mini Cooper to victory in the Monte Carlo Rally in 1964 it was the first of a hat-trick of Mini successes in the event. It was completely classless, and was driven by students and millionaires alike. It captured the public imagination, unlike its modern successor which, despite its many gaudy coats of paint, does not have the style and charisma of its predecessor. *(E.S. Gosling collection)*

John Gosling is pictured here, in 1904, at Halsdon House, Luppitt, in a fine Edwardian landaulet. This was a limousine, the roof of which was flexible at the rear, and folded down if desired. *(E.S. Gosling collection)*

This Ford Popular van with a 1172cc side valve engine was used by the Beer Stone Co., *c.* 1939. During the Second World War, with leaded petrol, this model would burn out exhaust valves every 10,000 miles, and you would be lucky to get the crown wheel and pinion to last for more than 30,000 miles. (*Colyford Motor Museum*)

Opposite, top: Ted Gosling is pictured here with his 1928 vintage Singer 8, outside his parents' house in Eyewell Green, Seaton, 1956. Although the vehicle had been in store since 1939, it only required a few minor adjustments to make it roadworthy. He sold the car on in an unrestored state and many years later, much to his delight, he came upon it, fully restored and looking splendid, at a Taunton vintage car rally. (*E.S. Gosling collection*)

Opposite, bottom: In Devon the growth of motoring was unstoppable and by 1930 most towns and villages had a garage. Martin & Staddon, featured in this advertisement, were motor engineers in Budleigh Salterton and were agents for Dodge cars. (*E.S. Gosling collection*)

This pre-war Ford Anglia was photographed in Devon during the Second World War. You can see the regulation black-out headlamp masks. *(J. Hooper)*

Opposite, top: The Vauxhall Iron Works Ltd made its first car in 1903, a tiller-steered one-cylinder 6hp runabout. The 1939 Vauxhall seen here in North Devon was used on war work during the Second World War. Note the black-out masks on the headlights. *(Colyford Motor Museum)*

Opposite, bottom: The Morris Minor Traveller car seen here proved to be a popular means of transport throughout Devon before the 1970s. The reasonable initial cost and roominess, combined with the Morris Minor's well-known attributes of economy, performance and roadholding, made this small station wagon an attractive proposition for the family man or businessman. *(Colyford Motor Museum)*

Frank Elston (right), with the War Production team at Helliers Garage, Honiton, during the Second World War. (*E.S. Gosling collection*)

By 1928 the firm of Morris Motors was the biggest manufacturer in Britain, building 20,000 cars a year out of the country's total production of 55,000. One of William Morris's most popular cars was the Morris Cowley, the model pictured here near Princetown. (*E.S. Gosling collection*)

The 3-litre Bentley seen here, still resplendent some thirty years after it was made, is being admired by Derek Gould and Sandra Moore from Sidmouth, who were visiting a vintage car rally in the 1960s. *(E.S. Gosling collection)*

The village of Beer is strangely empty in this picture from 1928. The Bullnose Morris parked in the street adds to the period feel of the photograph. *(Seaton Museum)*

During the past thirty years local authorities in Devon have seen an increasing number of complaints about the effect cars have had on the environment. Motorists and non-motorists alike complain about the clogging of the roads by cars, and shoppers are wearied by the problem of finding parking spaces. But take a look back to the past. The top picture shows the old road between Torquay and Paignton at Chelston in 1871, taken long before the car changed our way of life. It was even better in the 1950s (left) when you can see in this picture of Woodville Road, Exmouth, c. 1956, that a Morris Minor found parking easy. (*E.S. Gosling collection*)

Traffic during the peak holiday periods, and heavy goods vehicles all the year round, caused serious congestion in Okehampton, making the construction of the bypass necessary. The problem was where to build it: to the north of the town through good farmland, or to the south through the northern edge of the Dartmoor National Park. The process by which the final route was chosen was complicated and lengthy, until finally the southern route through part of the National Park was selected. In the top picture a wave from Roads Minister, Mr Peter Bottomley, marks the start of the work on the Okehampton Bypass, 17 November 1986. Below, Torridge and West Devon MP Emma Nicholson cuts a ribbon to officially open the second carriageway of the new bypass, 22 December 1988. *(Express & Echo)*

J. Tolman's Cycle Depot in Colyton, *c.* 1904. Mr Tolman's cycle depot displays a confusion of signs and advertisements, including the interesting Pratts Motor Spirit sign. The early motorist in Devon invariably carried a spare can of petrol. Garages were almost unknown, and depots like Tolman's would sell petrol in 2-gallon cans. (*Seaton Museum*)

A wonderfully evocative photograph looking up Castle Hill, Axminster, taken by Kenneth Harman-Young during September 1904. The children seen here look charming, and the street was then a place where they could play in safety. (*Seaton Museum*)

Looking up Bampton Street, Tiverton, from the Palmerston corner, *c.* 1958. This photograph was taken before local authorities chose to use gallons of yellow paint on kerbs to ban waiting, and Devon town streets were still reasonably free of traffic congestion. *(Express & Echo)*

A street scene in Tiverton before the days of the dreaded yellow lines, and at a time when the traffic flow could go in either direction, *c.* 1959. Note the Ford Zephyr parked beside the right-hand pavement, and the Morris Oxford coming down the street. *(Express & Echo)*

This fine Lancia Lambda photographed in the Ham car park, Sidmouth, in 1958, belonged to Ted Gosling, who bought the car for only £75. The Lambda, with a V-4 engine of 2.1 litres and independent front suspension, was introduced in 1923 by Vincenzo Lancia, the famous Italian racing driver who became a car manufacturer. It was really a most advanced car, with an alloy cylinder block, pump cooling, and a unitary body chassis. About 13,000 Lambdas were built before 1931. Ted, on the right road, could hit 75mph with this car. *(E.S. Gosling collection)*

Opposite, top: East Street, Ashburton, on a wet day during March 1961. The cars seen here are the A30 and the MG saloon; both were typical cars of that period. *(E.S. Gosling collection)*

Opposite, bottom: Townsend Garage, Beer, *c.* 1938. The author left school during the Second World War at the age of fourteen to commence a five-year apprenticeship in this garage. During the first year his weekly wage was *7s 6d. (G. Oborn)*

For more than a hundred years the ideal present for a young boy was a model motor car. In the top picture we have what must be one of the earliest toy cars in Devon. This model was made by Mr Tucker of Bovey Tracey in 1902 for his young son. The boy in the bottom picture (*c. 1930*) certainly looks thrilled to be sitting in this splendid pedal car with rubber tyres, the horseshoe radiator reminiscent of a Bugatti. (*Colyford Motor Museum*)

6

Motor Sport

Motorcycle trials are events in which a cross-country course has to be completed within a certain time, with points lost on observed sections of the course for stopping or touching the ground. With sheer determination and concentration Gerald Oborn from Beer makes his way up an observed section in a Devon trial on his BSA trials bike, *c.* 1965. *(G. Oborn)*

Well-known East Devon motorcycle trials competitor Gerald Oborn is seen here battling through mud and water on his BSA trials bike, *c.* 1965. *(G. Oborn)*

Paul Richards from Paignton stands beside his self-prepared Vauxhall Nova 1400cc, *c.* 1995. *(R. Richards)*

These are trophies won by Paul Richards, who was a regular competitor around the south-west in the 1990s, competing in his self-prepared Vauxhall Nova 1400cc. Taking part in sprints/hill climbs and tarmac stage rallying resulted in Association of South West Motor Clubs Championship wins in 1994 and 1996 and the ASWMC Tarmac Stage Rally overall Championship win in 2001. The Championship winning car was then sold to finance the building of a new current model Vauxhall Corsa 1600cc rally car, which is due for completion in 2006. *(R. Richards)*

George Trevett, the well-known Seaton garage owner, is pictured here in 1937, setting off for a motorcycle trial. *(E.S. Gosling collection)*

A competitor in a trials special gets ready to tackle an observed section in a pre-war London to Exeter trial, *c.* 1938. *(Colyford Motor Museum)*

Garage owner George Trevett, standing on the right, was acting as a marshal on an observed section of the London to Exeter Trial, *c.* 1938. The car ready to tackle the section looks like a Hillman Minx. *(Colyford Motor Museum)*

Gerald Oborn tackles the water section in an Otter Vale motorcycle trial. *(G. Oborn)*

Mr W.F. (Bill) Barnard, proprietor of the Anchor Garage, Axminster, leads the way as champion driver Erik Carlsson and his co-driver Mr G. Palm (carrying bag) walk into the garage for a brief rest during the RAC International Rally of Great Britain on 15 November 1963. The garage was the last control point in this rally in which Mr Carlsson, driving a Saab, took third place. (*Colyford Motor Museum*)

The Ford team doing speedy maintenance work on Pat Moss's Cortina while it was at the Anchor Garage, Axminster, the last control point in the RAC International Rally, 15 November 1963. Watching the work is (in shirtsleeves, second from left) Mr Robin Barnard, son of Bill Barnard, who ran the National Benzole garage. (*Colyford Motor Museum*)

Miss Pat Moss and her co-driver, Miss J. Nadin, leaving their Ford Cortina for a brief spell of relaxation after putting in at the Anchor Garage, Axminster, 15 November 1963. Pictured with them is Mr Bill Barnard, proprietor of the National Benzole garage. *(Colyford Motor Museum)*

Pat Moss is pictured driving her Ford Cortina, leaving the control point at the Anchor Garage, Axminster, during the RAC Rally, 15 November 1963. *(Colyford Motor Museum)*

A group of interested spectators admire two of the competing cars at Wiscombe Park Hill Climb, *c.* 1958. *(E.S. Gosling collection)*

The chain-driven Morgan three-wheelers built at Malvern, Worcestershire, by a family firm founded in 1910, were widely known as Moggies. The Morgan seen here with the 10/40 JAP engine was making its way up an observed section in East Devon during a pre-war London to Exeter trial. *(Colyford Motor Museum)*

Couchill Hill Climb, near Beer, *c.* 1936. Couchill was a popular venue for motorcycling events, which included hill climbs and scrambles, from the 1920s until just after the Second World War. This competitor is riding a Royal Enfield. *(E.S. Gosling collection)*

During the 1930s hill climbs for motorbikes became a popular sport for the enthusiast. At Couchill, during the summer of 1936, spectators gather to watch a competitor tackle the hill. *(E.S. Gosling collection)*

Wiscombe Park Hill Climb, *c.* 1958. Wiscombe Park, between Seaton and Sidmouth, is beautifully situated about a mile from Southleigh. The drive to the house was first used as a hill climb in the 1950s. In the top picture spectators are admiring a Bugatti, one of the competing cars. Ettore Bugatti was born in Italy, and built cars with the precision of fine watches. These cars, with their distinctive horseshoe radiator grille and tearing-calico exhaust note, dominated motor sport in the 1920s. In the bottom picture a competitor at Wiscombe reaches the finishing line. *(E.S. Gosling collection)*

7

Other Means of Transport

Cutting timber at The Wessiters, Seaton, 1904. Mr W.H. Head and his employees
are cutting timber with a large circular saw, driven by a steam traction engine.
This engine travelled from the farms to the estates and the outfit included a
small caravan, known as 'the box', in which the two drivers lived.
(E.S. Gosling collection)

This 1908 Levis motorcycle was ridden by a Colyton man until 1922. The motorcycle was then stored in a garden shed until 1959, when it was bought by Ted Gosling for £3. It was finally sold on to a main London motorcycle dealer, who restored the machine. (*E.S. Gosling collection*)

On Devon roads motor accidents are inevitable and date back to the days when cars first became a means of transport. This accident occurred on the Musbury road, near Axminster, *c.* 1933. A group of interested cyclists gather to watch the police. The van belonged to Eastmans the butchers. (*E.S. Gosling collection*)

Passengers alight from a Jersey Air Line Douglas DC3 Dakota at Exeter Airport on a wet day in August 1961. *(E.S. Gosling collection)*

The RNLI, which was formed in 1824, provides a much needed but very different form of transport around the coast of Devon. The skill and courage of the volunteer crews have resulted in many lives being saved. The *George and Sarah Strachan* lifeboat, seen here, was going to a call-out at Exmouth, *c.* 1960. *(E.S. Gosling collection)*

The Grand Western Canal was built in 1814 at Tiverton, primarily for the use of the lime trade. It was in operation for over 130 years and its remaining 11 miles run through some of the prettiest countryside in Devon. Jim the shire horse can be seen pulling the narrowboat to its summer stopping place on the Tiverton Canal Basin, *c.* 1990. On the boat are members of the Grand Western Canal Trust. *(Express & Echo)*

Jim the shire horse is seen here about to pull the Butty narrowboat, *Bodmin*, to its summer stopping place at the Tiverton Canal Basin. This is another trip for members of the Grand Western Canal Trust, August 1994. *(Express & Echo)*

Boat trips offer one of the best ways to explore the spectacular coastline between Torquay and Seaton. From the latter part of the nineteenth century to the present day visitors and residents alike have enjoyed these sea trips. In the top picture, taken in June 1904, the pleasure steamer the *Duchess of Devonshire*, conveying passengers from Weymouth to Torquay, makes a stop at Seaton. In the lower picture, and exactly 100 years later, a Stuart Line cruiser arrives at Seaton beach, 12 June 2004. (*Top: E.S. Gosling collection; Bottom: Colin Bowerman*)

Ted Gosling can be seen here installing a new engine in one of Bradfords' Bedford lorries, 1952. Bradfords, still trading in Devon today, supplied coal and coke, corn and building materials. *(E.S. Gosling collection)*

Tiverton High School pupils are pictured here alongside the vehicle with which they reached the 1998 South-West and Wales regional final. From left to right: Michael Phillips (15), Trevor Mills, sales manager of Richardson of Tiverton, Matthew Bard (15), David Lacey, service manager of Richardson of Tiverton, Jack Vanstone (15), Edward Smith (16), and, seated, Paul Crease, head of technology at the school. *(Express & Echo)*

You can see from this picture, taken at Dunkeswell in 1975, that the Royal Marines at Lympstone had a different type of transport. *(E.S. Gosling collection)*

Below: Great excitement at Rousdon Manor on 20 July 1929, when a bi-plane made a forced landing on the lawn of the Manor House. Estate workers and local farmhands group together by the biplane for a souvenir picture. *(Norman Lambert collection)*

Reginald Wilkie Gosney sits proudly on his tricycle in this charming Edwardian photograph, taken in 1903. Gosney, the son of an East Devon chemist, was killed on active service in Mesopotamia during the First World War. *(E.S. Gosling collection)*

Above: Cyclists had, of course, been using Devon roads rather longer than motorists, and the invention of the safety bicycle and the pneumatic tyre made cycling an activity for both sexes. This happy group of cyclists was caught by the camera in 1925, just before they set off from Torquay to explore the Devon lanes. *(E.S. Gosling collection)*

This young Axmouth boy, John Widger, appears to be enjoying the ride on his father's bicycle, although it would have been frowned on by the law (*c.* 1970). *(J. Richards)*

Such a sight we will never see again. Hancock's, the fairground people from Bristol, are manoeuvring a Burrell traction engine, no. 1740, around the Overgang hairpin bend at Brixham in 1904. The traction engine is towing the centre truck for the four-abreast set of gallopers (a kind of roundabout). *(David James)*

A soggy reception for Anderton & Rowlands travelling cinema on 15 August 1906. Crowds gather to watch the fine traction engine cross the ford at the Old Mill, Sidmouth. *(R. Richards)*

By the beginning of the twentieth century machinery was coming into use on the land in Devon. Traction engines toured the county under their own steam, for hire on different farms. The engine seen here belonged to Mr Asa Richards, and was working at Reynolds Farm, Beer, *c.* 1902. *(R. Richards)*

Robert Miller, who lived near Sidmouth, is pictured here at the controls of his own traction engine, *c.* 1975. The photograph was taken at the Steam Laundry in Sidford, when his help was enlisted after the laundry machinery had broken down. *(R. Richards)*

During the Second World War Devon experienced a different form of transport, when aircrew from local airfields carried bombs to drop on Germany. Dunkeswell was home to the US Navy Air Arm Wing 7, and these American aircrew are briefing in front of a PB4Y (known as a Liberator). *(E.S. Gosling collection)*

A newer form of transport, and a good way to obtain a fine view of the county, is by hang-glider. Nick Sharples can be seen here with his hang-glider in the football field at Colyton, *c.* 1990. *(Seaton Museum)*

The penny-farthing, with a vast wheel in front and a tiny one behind, seemed acutely perilous, and the author, Ted Gosling, can confirm this. Here he is in 1959, riding a penny-farthing along the Sidmouth Esplanade, for Sidmouth carnival. *(E.S. Gosling collection)*

This fine study of a woman cyclist in Barnstaple, taken during the Edwardian period, proves that many of the early objections to women riders were forgotten, and bicycling for the ladies had gained a new respectability. *(E.S. Gosling collection)*

A Morris Cowley for 6*d*! Devon hotelier Mr Herbert Arthur Good is pictured here with the car he won in 1933 in a raffle at a Conservative Party fête at Lord Clinton's seat, Bicton. The draw ticket for the car cost 6*d*. (*Seaton Museum*)

Bovey Tracey carnival tableau, *c.* 1930. The colourful spectacle of the carnival was as much a part of the Devon calendar as the seasons of sowing, harvest and Christmas. Transport played an important part in the festival, and here the local Excelsior garage has entered this decorated car in the carnival. (*Colyford Motor Museum*)

The chain-drawn bicycle with pneumatic tyres was developed in the 1880s. At first it was a novelty for the well off, until mass production brought the cost down and made it the main means of transport for the working class. This picture was taken in Sidmouth in 1885, when the new lifeboat arrived for its launch. The lady bicyclists leading the procession must have found their voluminous skirts something of a liability, but these were the correct clothes to wear at that time. *(E.S. Gosling collection)*

The village of Whimple became world famous as the home of Whiteway's famous Devon Cyders. The fleet of motor lorries pictured here at Whimple in about 1936 were used for deliveries by the firm. (*Colyford Motor Museum*)

The goat, which still roams wild in mountainous regions, was one of the first animals to be domesticated, and although few are kept on Devon farms many smallholders keep them to produce milk and cheese. Back in 1933 this goat was kept for a different purpose, and here a young boy is enjoying a ride on the Seaton Burrow in a goat cart. (*Seaton Museum*)

The worst disaster in living memory to hit East Devon came at about 3 a.m. on 1 October 1960, when 3in of rain cascaded down. Within minutes the centuries-old village of Axmouth, lying on the River Axe, the ancient town of Colyton, bordered by the River Coly, and the tiny village of Whitford were swimming in water. Even in these dreadful conditions transport of a sort carried on. In the top picture an Express Dairies milk lorry is tackling the floods on the road from Road Green, Colyton, and in the bottom picture, also near Road Green, the local farmer in his tractor seems to be taking it all in his stride. (*Tony Byrne-Jones*)

It was in 1955 that Christopher Cockerell patented an idea for a craft using downwards-directed fans to raise it off the ground, while the propellers of a single engine drove the vessel forward with a minimum of friction, over ground or water. Although a ferry service with a hovercraft to cross the English Channel began in 1968, no such service ever existed in Devon. From time to time, however, they did make a quick visit to the East and South Devon coastal towns. Here in 1974 we have a hovercraft landing on Seaton beach, which caused great excitement in the town. (*Seaton Museum*)

In the 1920s few women rode motorcycles, and I suspect these girls astride a BSA were posing for a picture on a boyfriend's machine. The photograph was taken in Exmouth on 7 August 1929. (*J. Hooper*)

The long coastline of Devon, north and south, and its many estuaries and harbours, have combined to make commerce by sea play an important role in Devon transport. Unfortunately shipwrecks did occur, and here we have the *Malpas Belle*, a Polish-registered barque laden with iron ore, which was wrecked, with no loss of life, between Seaton and Beer during a storm in February 1922. *(E.S. Gosling collection)*

A wet winter's day on Woodbury Common, *c.* 1930. Looking at the state of the pony and trap, the people pictured here were probably following a hunt. *(Seaton Museum)*

At the end of the First World War Seaton builder George Henry Richards purchased a pre-war chain-driven car and had it converted into a pickup lorry. The vehicle had solid rubber tyres, and the top speed with a heavy load was about 10mph. T7084 is seen here just after the conversion and ready for the road – it would certainly be a wonderful addition to a vintage lorry collection today. This pick-up lorry gave the building firm many years of reliable service before being exchanged for a more modern vehicle. (*Colyford Motor Museum*)

Another of those fine documentary photographs that show the closed-off, private working world of the traction engine repair shop. J.R. Pratt had his premises in Chardstock, and in this picture you can see a corner of his traction engine and boiler repair shop, *c.* 1915. (*Norman Lambert collection*)

Trevett's breakdown lorry pictured in 1957 outside Trevett's filling station on Harbour Road, Seaton. The site is now occupied by the Rainbow complex. *(E.S. Gosling collection)*

The St John Ambulance men seen here looking very smart were attending the dedication of the first motor ambulance in Seaton, *c.* 1938. Originally a Chrysler car belonging to Dr James of the Ryalls Court School, it was given to the town, and converted to an ambulance by A. Dowell and Sons of Exeter. Mr H.F. Norcombe, the wartime Chairman of Seaton Council, is standing on the left, next to Mr Harry Clapp. *(E.S. Gosling collection)*

Torbay is a favoured retirement area for the country's senior citizens, resulting in an ever-increasing number of mobility scooters. Ron Taylor, a resident of the Bethesda residential home in Torquay, is seen here in August 1997 enjoying the freedom these scooters provide for the elderly. *(J. Hooper)*

Although goods transport by lorries is often maligned by the motorist, nevertheless lorries play an essential part in the Devon economy. In the top picture is a goods lorry operated by M. Tregaskis from Seaton station, *c.* 1939. In the lower picture lorries from Bass Worthington line up in Exmouth in 1956. (*E.S. Gosling collection*)

ACKNOWLEDGEMENTS

I am grateful to all those who have helped in the compilation of this book by contributing valuable information. Particular thanks must go to Robin Barnard of the Colyford Motoring Memories Museum, for allowing me to use pictures and contributing valuable information.

David James from Brixham gave much help, and I am grateful for the pictures loaned to me by Roderick Richards. Many of the railway photographs came from Mike Clement's collection, and Mike also contributed much valuable information.

I am indebted to the following people for allowing me to use photographs belonging to them: Colin Bowerman, *Express & Echo*, Seaton Museum, Norman Lambert, A. Hooper, Down's Motors of Ottery St Mary, Daphne Harman Young, Dart Pleasure Craft Ltd, Gerald Oborn and Colin Brown of Seaton Tramway.

Many books, newspapers and organisations were consulted, too many to mention, but the following were a mine of information: *Express & Echo*, *Western Morning News*, *History of the Motor Car* by Peter Roberts, *Devon* by W.G. Hoskins, *Devon Railways* by M. Clement and *British Sports Cars* by Gregor Grant.

Thanks must go to Lyn Marshall, whose help made this book possible, to my wife Carol for her encouragement, and to Simon Fletcher and Michelle Tilling of Sutton Publishing.

The accuracy of the facts in this book have been checked as carefully as possible. However, original sources can contain errors, and memories fade over the years.

The Austin van, pictured here at Whitford outside the Hare & Hounds, *c.* 1959, was a useful workhorse at that time.
This pub closed in about 1970 and is now a private house.
(*E.S. Gosling collection*)